Active
Workplace 911

An expert guide to preventing, preparing for and prevailing over attacks at work, school and church

By Vaughn Baker and Mark Warren
Strategos International

Dedication

In memory of the victims who have perished or suffered as a result of workplace violence. May this book help prevent another tragedy.

Table of Contents

ABOUT THE AUTHORS

VAUGHN BAKER

Vaughn Baker is president of Strategos International, a Kansas City, Mo.,-based firm that provides security training, consulting and executive protection services.

Baker has 20 years of experience in law enforcement including patrol, investigation, SWAT and special operations. He has trained thousands of school, health care, government, law enforcement and military personnel in security practices. Baker has also developed specialized intruder response curriculum for schools and churches, including some of the nation's leading training on behavior pattern recognition. He is the author of "The Church Security Handbook."

In addition, he served as an instructor and deputy director of training for the Surefire Institute, a California-based tactical lighting manufacturer and tactical training company.

Baker is also the director of security for a church of more than 7,500 members in the Kansas City area, a position he has held for more than a decade.

MARK WARREN

Mark Warren is executive vice president and director of training for Strategos International. He served in law enforcement in multiple jurisdictions including the Blue Springs, Mo., Police Department, where he finished his career with the rank of sergeant. Warren also worked as an undercover officer for the Jackson County, Mo., Drug Task Force. Before joining civilian law enforcement, Warren served in the U.S. Army as a military police officer. He has trained thousands of students in security through Strategos, the Surefire Institute and the Western Missouri Public Safety Institute. Other career highlights include:

- Field operational work during crises.

- International security missions in the service of faith-based organizations.

- Managing security at large events.

- Serving on his church's security team.

Authors' Note

This book is intended to address threats to all types of organizations: businesses, schools, houses of worship, non-profits, government agencies and others. For sake of simplicity, we use the term "workplace" to address all of them.

– Vaughn Baker and Mark Warren

ABOUT STRATEGOS INTERNATIONAL

Strategos International is an innovative leader in security training, consulting and protective services. The firm focuses on protecting people and property during times of crisis.

Strategos has trained more than 150,000 people in 15 countries since its founding in 2002. Training clients have included personnel in schools, businesses, non-profits, churches, law enforcement and the U.S. military.

In addition to training, Strategos provides:

- Protective services.

- Facility security surveys.

- Surveillance and investigation.

- Security planning and consulting.

- Expert witness testimony.

Learn more at www.strategosintl.com.

It *Can* Happen Here
But does it have to?

"Fortune favors the prepared mind." – Louis Pasteur

"He could have been anyone, going anywhere."

That's how the Cincinnati Enquirer[1] introduced the shooter who terrorized a bustling downtown business district on a midweek morning in 2018.

"He blended into the crowd, moving among the bankers and accountants and lawyers and clerks and secretaries as if he were one of them. As if he belonged.

"But he didn't."

The 29-year-old certainly *seemed* to fit the mold of the other workers making their way into the Cincinnati office tower. He sipped coffee, was dressed in business casual attire and had a typical work bag slung over his shoulder.

But only he knew it was not filled with a laptop or lunch. Instead, the satchel held 250 rounds of ammunition and a 9 mm handgun.

Finished with his coffee, this nonchalant onlooker walked into the Fifth Third Bank Center ... and opened fire.

---

[1] Cincinnati Enquirer: "4 minutes, 28 seconds: How the Cincinnati shooting unfolded" https://cin.ci/2N8O6k2

For the next four-and-a-half minutes, people screamed, glass shattered and bodies hit the floor. Hundreds of calls poured into 911 dispatch.

The shooter fired at people as they ran and as they dove for cover. He riddled an elevator door with bullets as it closed.

Three were dead, two were wounded and more seemed destined to die.

But as a squad of police closed in on the killer, the next death was his own. Officers spotted him through a window and unleashed a volley of bullets and a torrent of shattering glass.

It was over.

"We never expected something like this to materialize on our doorstep the way that it did," said Fifth Third Bank CEO Greg Carmichael. "We'll learn from this and get better and be stronger."[2]

Carmichael's sentiment can instruct anyone who is responsible for the safety of others.

First, don't be caught off guard by the reality of violence in the workplace, schools and public places. Second, learn from others and do everything in your power to prevent an attack from taking place – or happening again.

---

[2] Cincinnati Enquirer: "Cincinnati shootings: Fifth Third CEO tells America 'This has to stop'" https://cin.ci/2xXG3Rn

Yes, but that was there (not here)

Our need for psychological self-preservation leads us to think, "Yeah, but it couldn't, or wouldn't, happen here."

Unfortunately, these attacks have no signature method, making them nearly impossible to predict. They occur at Wal-Marts and Waffle Houses, at one-room schools and on sprawling college campuses. The only consistency seems to be randomness.

That means, yes, it could happen to you. Or to us.

There is no ironclad plan to stop an attack at your school, church or workplace. After all, despite world-class protection, global leaders are assassinated. But regardless of those limitations, there's still much you can do. It might mean starting with something as simple as locking the door and asking, "Who's there?" before letting someone in.

This small measure alone could save lives – maybe your own.

If not you, who? If not now, when?

Anyone who has lived through a shooting is left to ponder what could have been. Were there warning signs? Could it have been stopped? "What if I had ...?" That's especially true if you're responsible for employees, students or a congregation. We can't rewind the tape. But we can make decisions today that will impact tomorrow.

Even indecision is a decision. It starts with a choice to act, defer or deny. Which option will you choose?

CHAPTER 1

Intruder Violence:
Coming to a Place Near You
Who's at risk and what are the odds?

"A prudent person foresees danger and takes precautions." – Proverbs 22:3, The Bible

We're not alarmists.

Alarmism is exaggerating fears to cause anxiety and get attention (or business). It might work in the short term, but in the long run it's like crying wolf. People stop listening because the credibility of the town crier has been compromised.

So let's be clear: It's unlikely an attacker will shoot up your workplace, school or house of worship.

It's also unlikely those places will be destroyed by fire, washed away in a flood or obliterated by a tornado. Yet we go to great pains to protect ourselves from these unlikely events.

Unlikely, however, does not mean unthinkable.

There were 28 mass attacks in 2017 alone, according to the U.S. Secret Service.[3]

- They occurred in locations as diverse as New York City and Clovis, N.M.

- 42 percent occurred at businesses.

- 32 percent occurred in public spaces, such as parks or concerts.

- 19 percent occurred in schools or churches.

The long-term impact of workplace violence is even more sobering. The FBI reports 250 active shooter incidents between 2000-2016, resulting in 2,217 deaths.[4] That's an average of one homicide every three days.

To make wise decisions about security we must not only consider the odds of being attacked. We also have to assess the impact of being unprepared.

Objection: But we're different
It's likely you have a great corporate culture and people enjoy working at your organization. The thought of an employee showing up with a gun seems inconceivable. But this sentiment misunderstands the reality of on-the-job attacks.

---

[3] U.S. Secret Service: "Mass Attacks in Public Spaces 2017" https://bit.ly/2pQRvei
[4] FBI: "Quick Look: 250 Active Shooter Incidents in the United States From 2000 to 2017" https://bit.ly/2NzfZpL

In some ways, the phrase "workplace violence" could be considered a misnomer. It implies the violence is caused by or related to a job. Most of the time, however, the workplace is simply the location.

The majority of shootings are motivated by factors outside of employment – chiefly conflicts in personal relationships.

Domestic violence: It leaves home

One in four women report being victims of domestic violence. An employee may have split from her domestic partner and moved to an unlisted address. *But her ex knows where she works.*

Numerous shootings start with this scenario. And when they happen, people outside the conflict are often caught in the crossfire.

Stylist Chantille Truss went to work on a Friday morning, not realizing it was the last day of her life. Her estranged husband drove to her suburban Kansas City salon and opened fire, killing her in full view of employees and customers. Later that morning he was found dead in his vehicle from a self-inflicted gunshot wound.[5]

---

[5] U.S. News & World Report: "Police: Man Fatally Shoots Wife at Salon, Kills Himself" https://bit.ly/2xYEvXs

The U.S. Secret Service analyzed 2017's mass attacks[6] and found the killers' motives stemmed from these sources:

- Workplace: 21 percent
- Ideological or racial: 21 percent
- Domestic: 18 percent
- Mental health: 14 percent
- Personal: 7 percent
- Other: 18 percent

Only one in five incidents stemmed from a workplace grievance. Even if you could successfully address every in-house problem, 80 percent of incidents are still fueled by factors outside the office. What are some of the more common outside triggers? They include:

- Failing relationships at home, in extended families or in social life.
- Financial pressure.
- Child custody disputes and other post-divorce conflicts.

---

[6] U.S. Secret Service: "Mass Attacks in Public Spaces 2017" https://bit.ly/2pQRvei

In addition, an attitude of victimhood, also referred to as a "martyr complex," can lead employees to compile a lengthy list of grievances until their psyche ruptures and they resort to violence.

Who are the shooters?
In addition to learning their motivations, we also need to understand the identity of potential attackers. They aren't just the people under your roof – or even their family members. They could be:

- Criminals with no connection to your workplace. If an employee discovers a burglary in process, violence may ensue.

- Disgruntled customers or vendors.

- Former employees, including those who were terminated or laid off.

- Ideological attackers (political, religious, anti-religious).

Workplace triggers
Although most shootings are not directly related to the workplace, some certainly are.

Our increasingly competitive marketplace can create an environment that breaks the psychological "last straw."

Triggering events include:

- Layoffs and fear of them.

- Reorganizations, mergers and changing technology.

- Economic downturns.

- Employee reprimands or poor performance reviews.

- Difficulty in interpersonal relationships.

- Abusive management.

- Understaffing and overwork.

Where do attacks happen?

Since most attacks do not discriminate, profiling shooters and preventing assaults is often a puzzle.

Active shooters destroy stereotypes.

The three-person auto-body shop is at risk as well as the 400-employee back office.

Active shooters destroy stereotypes. For example, conventional wisdom holds that small towns are safe and big cities are dangerous.

In fact, mass shootings are more likely to occur in towns of fewer than 10,000 residents than in urban areas.[7] They

---

[7] The Final Report and Findings of the Safe Schools Initiative, U.S. Department of Education and U.S. Secret Service, https://bit.ly/2avgjlw

can even happen at a lawnmower manufacturing plant in small-town Kansas.[8]

That's where an employee of Excel Industries in Hesston (population 3,709) went on a multi-city commute of terror, killing three people and wounding 14. After shooting an elderly woman in the company parking lot, he stormed inside and continued his assault.

A witness said the gunman "came in through that back door, where assembly is, and just started spraying his AK at everybody, just shooting random people."

The attacker even shot the city's responding chief of police. But Doug Schroeder battled through his injury and returned fire, killing the gunman.

The bottom line?
In less than a minute, your office, school or house of worship can become a crime scene. If you could do something, would you?

---

[8] The Guardian: "Gunman who killed three in Kansas shooting named by police" https://bit.ly/2NNXEGg

CHAPTER 2

Assessing the Threat: Locations and Risks

Different types of organizations face unique security challenges. Here's what they're up against.

"Just look at that giant door — we've got four of them. ... You can't make that totally airtight safe, no matter what." – Joe, UPS employee[9]

Every organization could save time, money and lives if there were a cookie-cutter approach to security. But schools, churches and workplaces have vastly different security needs and risks.

Businesses alone have wide-ranging vulnerabilities.

We'll start with them because, despite the media attention given to school attacks, most active shooter deaths occur on the job.

---

[9] San Francisco Chronicle: "Bay Area companies sharpen focus on security after shootings" https://bit.ly/2NSeGTT

Wreaking havoc at work
In 2016, more than one person was murdered in the workplace daily, leaving a body count of 500.[10]

And of course, real life doesn't follow the pace of statistics. Many may die in a single day or week. That's what happened in the fall of 2018 when 24 hours of workplace violence led to five deaths and 11 injuries across three states. The carnage hit a software company in Wisconsin, a government building in Pennsylvania and a distribution center in Maryland.[11]

Between 2000-2017, 56 percent of active shooter attacks occurred at businesses – nearly three times the rate of schools and six times the rate of churches.[12]

But "business" is a broad term. What are the risks and challenges specific to different types of workplaces? And how should each respond?

Back offices
These facilities are often unsigned and have minimal visitor traffic. As a result, they can be aggressive in their security by locking doors, screening entrants and requiring

---

[10] U.S. Bureau of Labor Statistics: "TED: The Economics Daily - There were 500 workplace homicides in the United States in 2016" https://bit.ly/2Qhi33d
[11] The Baltimore Sun: "Maryland Rite Aid shooting is third workplace shooting in 24 hours" https://bsun.md/2NMyAzj
[12] FBI: "Quick Look: 250 Active Shooter Incidents in the United States from 2000 to 2017" https://bit.ly/2NzfZpL

identification. However, administrative facilities are vulnerable to the same internal threats all businesses face:

- Spillover from domestic violence.

- Mental health-fueled assaults.

- Ideological attacks.

- Workplace grievances.

A threat that originates from an insider can be just as deadly as one that comes from outside the business.

Retail locations

Malls and department stores thrive on foot traffic – the more the merrier. Because screening and locking doors are not possible in these environments, tactics must shift to training employees to recognize potential threats. Retailers must also use preventative measures such as surveillance and security guards.

Industrial locations

Although they vary by industry, manufacturing plants and distribution centers often have a constant flow of deliveries. In addition, they may occupy dozens of acres and multiple buildings, slowing law enforcement's response to an attack.

This challenge was summed up by Joe, a UPS driver who spoke to the San Francisco Chronicle after an employee shot and killed three co-workers at a distribution center in 2017:

"Just look at that giant door — we've got four of them, and they're designed big and open because our trucks are going in and out all the time. You can't make that totally airtight safe, no matter what. It's like that in a lot of places, certainly not just ours. That's just the way it is."[13]

Because industrial locations are diverse, there's not a one-size-fits-all security plan. However, they can benefit from training employees to recognize threats, using surveillance cameras and managing the flow of people in and out of the site. The best approach is to create a security plan tailored for each facility.

Schools

Of all the attacks, offenses against teachers and children receive the most attention. And with good reason.

Schools are at the heart of our shared experience as a community. Our children, grandchildren and neighbors study in their classrooms and run on their playgrounds. We root for the home team, buy hot dogs at school carnivals and collaborate at PTA meetings.

Kids don't go to school to become commandos, but to learn to read, add, spell and run the bases.

---

[13] San Francisco Chronicle: "Bay Area companies sharpen focus on security after shootings" https://bit.ly/2NSeGTT

Schools are targeted by attackers from without and within. In addition to these vulnerabilities, educational institutions are subject to the same risks of any place of employment. For all these reasons, and more, school security is challenging.

While metal detectors have some value, they aren't panaceas. A determined shooter can simply move his attack to a location that's unscreened – a parking lot, foyer, bus or playground.

Hundreds or thousands of children arrive and depart our campuses daily. That's in addition to staff, parents and guests. All of them must be able to enter and exit without giving an opening to attackers. And there's always the possibility the shooter is a student or staff member who is lawfully inside.

Screening tools such as metal detectors can flag weapons, but their use is not universal. In addition, they can slow the entrance and exit of students to a crawl. While metal detectors have some value, they aren't panaceas. A determined shooter can simply move his attack to a location that's unscreened – a parking lot, foyer, bus or playground.

Many schools, particularly middle and high schools, employ police officers, often referred to as SROs (school resource officers). Many schools, though, can't afford them. And at any rate, one officer cannot adequately defend hundreds of students scattered across thousands of square feet.

Schools' best defense is a rigorous visitor management system and faculty trained in behavior recognition and emergency response. In the 4-10 minutes it takes police to arrive, the actions of teachers and staff may determine who lives and dies. Although the nature of schools does not allow them to become fortresses, many low-cost adaptations can be made. For example, simple modifications to doors can allow them to be swiftly secured. When an attacker encounters a barrier – such as a locked and reinforced door – he usually moves on to a softer target.

Houses of worship
Although there have always been attacks on churches in the United States, they have been rare until the last two decades.

- Between 1999-2017, the number of violent events at churches surged by 2,600 percent.

- There were 261 violent incidents in 2017.

- A total of 1,700 incidents occurred between 1999-2017.[14]

Churches, like schools, tug at our heartstrings. They're the location of weddings, baptisms, picnics and changed lives. But gunfire?

In this respect, houses of worship are no different from workplaces. They're often caught in the crossfire of circumstances they did not cause and cannot prevent.

"Take domestic discord, existential angst, mental illness, and the classic battle between good and evil and you have the most fertile ground for violence: church," writes Joel F. Shults, a trainer and former police chief.[15]

According to church security expert Carl Chinn[16], the top three reasons for violence at churches are:

1. Robbery

2. Domestic relational conflict

3. Personal conflict

---

[14] Carl Chinn, church security expert, speaker, media commentator and author of "Evil Invades Sanctuary." See www.CarlChinn.com and http://www.carlchinn.com/deadly-force-statistics.html.

[15] PoliceOne.com: "Faith groups: The hidden target of violence" https://bit.ly/2PBVQ3e

[16] Carl Chinn, church security expert, speaker, media commentator and author of "Evil Invades Sanctuary." See www.CarlChinn.com and http://www.carlchinn.com/deadly-force-statistics.html.

Perhaps the most infamous church shooting of all, the 2017 massacre in Sutherland Springs, Texas, has been linked to a family dispute.

Although ideological (anti-religious, political) attacks do occur, they account for fewer than 6 percent of incidents.

In addition, churches are soft targets because:

- They contain large crowds.

- These crowds are facing away from entrances and focused on activity at the front of the auditorium.

- These people are "sitting ducks" in a wide-open room and have no quick means of escape.

- Churches collect a cash offering – a tempting target.

The challenge for church security is maintaining a sense of reverence while being alert and responsive to intruders.

Houses of worship, perhaps even more than schools, want to avoid becoming fortresses. The DNA of churches can be summed up by lyrics from a traditional hymn:

Softly and tenderly Jesus is calling—
Calling for you and for me ...

Come home! come home!
Ye who are weary, come home!

Adding the line, *"Right after you step through the metal detector"* definitely affects the sense of the song and – more importantly – the image of the church.

Because of this sensitivity, the perception churches create is as important as the reality of their security strategy.

There is not a single right approach. Some churches choose an armed security presence, while others opt against this. In either case, *something* can be done to protect the congregation while maintaining its unique mission.

Security must become part of the mission of all ministries, not only the domain of an elite few.

Regardless of their stand on firearms, all churches can improve security by developing a culture of awareness. Houses of worship can no longer greet their visitors, close the doors and retire into sacred bliss in the auditorium. Eyes and ears must be engaged at all times.

Health care: risky business

Health care has the unfortunate distinction of being the No. 1 setting for workplace violence, accounting for 45 percent of all incidents.

- Between 40-75 percent of health care workers report being verbally or physically abused by patients or their families.[17]

- One in four nurses report experiencing on-the-job violence in the previous 12 months.[18]

- Workplace violence is four times more common in health care than in the rest of private industry.[19]

No matter the reason someone shows up at a health care facility, they bring along their personal baggage.

Hospitals, mental health facilities and other medical centers face a challenge similar to schools and houses of worship. They are places of trust and refuge people turn to for help and comfort in times of desperation. As a result, they are generally easy to access and often open 24 hours a day.

Because they are connected to crises, these facilities must exist with ever-present danger:

---

[17] U.S. News & World Report: "Violence in the Health Care Workplace" https://bit.ly/2fPZAuq

[18] Advisory Board consulting: "The alarming stats on violence against nurses" https://bit.ly/2xYRQ20

[19] OSHA: "Workplace Violence in Health Care" https://bit.ly/2dHRoZF

- Overdoses and abuse of prescription narcotics can result in patient violence.

- Suppressed family conflicts can erupt.

- Mental illness can lead to unpredictable behavior.

- In addition, medical facilities face the same threat of employee-based violence as other types of businesses.

No matter the reason someone shows up at a health care facility, they bring along their personal baggage. A level-one trauma center may be treating opposing gang members at the same time, not realizing family and friends of enemy factions are arriving in the waiting area.

"The environment is the perfect recipe for violence," according to U.S. News and World Report. "Patients feel poorly, are frightened and often face great uncertainty regarding their future. For family members, the stress can lead to disruptive and explosive behavior."[20]

Some health care facilities are using advanced scanners to detect weapons often missed by traditional metal detectors.

Many facilities employ private security. However, their level of training varies widely and many are unarmed.

---

[20] U.S. News & World Report: "Violence in the Health Care Workplace" https://bit.ly/2fPZAuq

The most important factor in protecting health care workers and patients is training. Medical staff need instruction in anticipating and responding to threats. Because each facility is unique, specific response plans are necessary.

Events and conferences: No more fun and games
Although some conferences and events have long been lightning rods for protests and occasional violence, these were somewhat predictable. Political and economic conferences are prime examples.

But in recent years, the randomness of violence at events has stunned the world of concert-goers, video game players and sports enthusiasts.

"Unpredictability is the new normal," reported Raconteur.[21]

Development Counsellors International, a travel marketing firm, reports security issues are "keeping event planners up at night."[22]

Wherever crowds gather, the potential for mass violence follows. Professional conferences are a ripe target.

---

[21] Raconteur: "Terrorist attacks are a constant threat for the events sector" https://bit.ly/2zEfoeu
[22] Associations Now: "Survey: Security, Costs Remain Pressure Points for Event Planners" https://bit.ly/2IDeO3z

The vast majority of these events are non-ideological and eschew politics. They're the quiet, mundane, but important gatherings of trade associations and hobbyists. Security is often an afterthought – if it's a thought at all.

Yet the same risks that affect the workplace, churches and schools can plague events of all sorts:

- There's a large, unguarded, unsuspecting population.

- Interpersonal and domestic conflicts can spill over into these environments.

- They can provide a spectacular "opportunity" for a mentally unstable killer to take numerous lives.

Event security is no longer optional. Failure to address risks may not only result in violence, but legal action.

In 2015, an ideologically radicalized couple killed 14 people in an attack on a meeting of San Bernardino (Calif.) County employees at the Inland Regional Center.

"To me, meetings are one big, giant hazard," consultant Joan Eisenstodt told Skift Global Forum, a travel industry organization. "There's nothing that isn't scary about them.

[Attending a meeting feels] like going home, so attendees believe that someone else is protecting them."[23]

Ground zero is Las Vegas, where a shooter killed 58 people and injured more than 800 as he fired from a hotel window into a crowd of 22,000 concertgoers in 2017. As of this writing, no motive has been discovered.[24]

But these violent events have also occurred at smaller venues, such as a video game tournament at a Florida bar, where a gunman killed two people and himself.[25]

Event security is no longer optional. Failure to address risks may not only result in violence, but legal action.

Each event is distinctive, so there is no one-size-fits all approach.

"Security must be properly integrated, but proportionality is key. Otherwise you will burn budgets and not be a lot more effective," Steve Cooper, former head of security for the Olympic Delivery Authority in London, told Raconteur.[26]

---

[23] Skift: "Event Security Takes on Fresh Importance for Meeting Planners" https://bit.ly/2uMpOID
[24] USA Today: "Las Vegas sheriff: Investigation into mass shooting shows no conspiracy or second gunman" https://usat.ly/2QIPu4X
[25] CNN: "Two killed in shooting at Jacksonville video game tournament" https://cnn.it/2MAl3u0
[26] Raconteur: "Terrorist attacks are a constant threat for the events sector" https://bit.ly/2zEfoeu

Despite the eclectic nature of events, all can benefit from:

- Visitor management systems, including mandatory ID.

- Video surveillance.

- Active security personnel, even trained volunteers.

- Restricting the number of entrances.

- Partnering with venues to enhance security.

Event planners also need to re-think previous practices in light of today's security challenges. In Las Vegas, fences were set up to restrict access to ticketholders. But when the attack started, those fences prevented concertgoers from escaping the killer.

What it means to you

Whether you're responsible for a school, a salon or a 25-acre distribution center, you're at risk. Your effectiveness at countering the threat depends on how well you understand and respond to the unique vulnerabilities of your facility and organization.

CHAPTER 3

The Attackers: Who Are They?

Understanding the threat is key to prevailing against it.

"Know thy self, know thy enemy. A thousand battles, a thousand victories." – Sun Tzu

We've established that, for the most part, a workplace attack doesn't depend on you. Someone may attack your organization even if:

- You rank in Fortune's "100 Best Companies to Work For."

- Your school has the state's best ACT scores.

- Your church gave away 20,000 meals to the homeless last year.

In other words, it's not you. *It's them.*

Patterns of mass attackers

If we're going to defeat our adversary, we have to understand him and have a response equal to the threat.

Law enforcement findings and our own research have determined that mass attackers:

- Want to set new body count records.

- Have a complete and total commitment to their cause.

- View themselves as victims and blame numerous people – often the entire world – for their personal failures.

- Are heavily armed but not highly trained.

- Generaly take no hostages.

We've also learned that they:

- Shoot victims repeatedly and at close range.

- Desire to share the personal space of their victims, much like serial killers.

- Have no escape plan and expect to die.

- Often commit suicide rather than become a perceived victim of law enforcement.

When we understand the extreme nature of the attacker, we gain insight into how we must prepare.

Seeking fame ... or infamy?

One motive unearthed in the aftermath of mass shootings is the attacker's desire for public adulation. Some killers believe if they can't have approval in life, they must seek it through death.

Many experts believe the intense media coverage surrounding individual shooters feeds their frenzy.

Trial attorney Wendy L. Patrick, author of "Red Flags: How to Spot Frenemies, Underminers, and Ruthless People," writes that active shooters have blurred the lines between fame and infamy in the quest for recognition: "The devastating 1999 Columbine High School shooting is an event that shocked the nation. Yet not everyone was horrified. Some were inspired."[27]

In dark corners of culture, a sympathetic group known as "The Columbiners" formed.

Patrick summarizes recent criminological and psychological research:

- In the last few decades, the number of mass shooters in pursuit of fame has multiplied.

- This type of shooter is found disproportionately in the United States.

- Fame-seeking shooters are younger and kill more people than others.

- School shooters often see themselves as victims of bullying, although they exaggerate the reality of their perceived abuse.

---

[27] Psychology Today: "What Motivates School Shooters?" https://bit.ly/2sjN6B8

At a basic level, an attack is an attack. But when we look deeper, there are differences in the motivations of those who bring harm to our workplaces.

"The shooters obsessed over being rejected by a perceived 'elite in-group' they view as having become successful unfairly. They thus plan to annihilate those who have transgressed against them in an act of vengeance for the way they were treated."

Types of attackers and intruders

At a basic level, an attack is an attack. But when we look deeper, there are differences in the motivations of those who bring harm to our workplaces.

Criminals

This intruder has no workplace connection and enters the property to commit robbery or another criminal act. Although violence may not be their goal, if discovered, they can turn lethal.

An 80-year-old volunteer at Central United Methodist Church in Wynne, Ark., was a victim of this fate. She interrupted a burglary when she went to the church for supplies. The burglar beat the woman to death with a cross from the altar.[28]

Employees and other insiders

This type of attacker can't be locked out because he comes from within. Employees, customers and service providers are in this category. They may retaliate for perceived unfair treatment or attack the workplace for unknown reasons.

The motive for a UPS worker's murder of three colleagues in 2017 has proven elusive. During one of the company's Wednesday Wellness meetings, he began firing the first of 20 rounds. As police arrived, he shot himself dead.[29]

While there were indications[30] the shooter believed he was bullied by his victims, the evidence is inconclusive. In addition, he had filed a grievance against UPS, protesting excessive overtime.

Customers, particularly in high-stakes professions, can also open the door to threats. In Arizona, six people connected to the legal profession were mysteriously gunned down in less than a week in 2018. The killings set

---

[28] WREG Memphis: "Man Convicted of Killing Woman With Cross In Church" https://bit.ly/2NKPSwK

[29] ABC News: "Victims of San Francisco UPS shooting appear to have been targeted, police say" https://abcn.ws/2zE4g1q

[30] KTVU: "San Francisco UPS shooting suspect believed he was being bullied by co-workers, sources say" https://bit.ly/2IoJuFr

the legal profession on edge, prompting the hiring of security guards and other security measures.[31]

The dead included a forensic psychiatrist, a psychologist and two paralegals. Some were connected, through their workplace, to the divorce of a man years earlier. Police said the killings appeared to be fueled by a grudge.

Although the attacker may only have one victim in mind, there is often collateral damage.

Domestic conflict attacker
This assailant has a personal, but strained, relationship with someone at the workplace. Although the attacker may only have one victim in mind, there is often collateral damage.

When those circumstances unfolded at a school in San Bernardino, Calif., the results were catastrophic.

Teacher Karen Elaine Smith was in her classroom with students at North Park Elementary School when her estranged husband abruptly entered. Without speaking, he fired 10 shots from a .357 Magnum. The dead included not

---

[31] AZCentral: "Six people killed by Scottsdale murder suspect, police say" https://bit.ly/2sG388N

only Karen Smith, but 8-year-old Jonathan Martinez. Anderson ended the siege by killing himself.[32]

Ideological attackers

These killers are motivated by dangerous ideas. They could be driven by religious, anti-religious, racist or political zeal. This attacker likely has no specific individual in mind. He desires to inflict mass casualties, whether by bullet or bomb.

Some of the most widely-known ideological attacks have been carried out by Islamic extremists. These include the Boston Marathon[33] bombing and the attack on county workers in San Bernardino, Calif.[34]

Political extremists include Timothy McVeigh, who blew up a federal building in Oklahoma City as an advocate of a radical anti-government philosophy.[35]

An ideological attacker may view a building as part of the infrastructure of government – therefore a legitimate target. Other facilities at risk could include courthouses, police stations and those involved in manufacturing

---

[32] The (San Bernardino) Sun: "'She was a spark of love': Teacher killed in San Bernardino school shooting remembered" https://bit.ly/2DBCYwk

[33] NPR: "Jury Will Hear Final Arguments in Sentencing of Boston Marathon Bomber" https://n.pr/2Oiv4Mz

[34] Desert Sun: "Year later, San Bernardino massacre leaves more questions than answers" https://desert.sn/2lnMC4G

[35] CNN: "Timothy McVeigh Profile" https://cnn.it/2OWRWyo

military equipment. Some killers may even feel justified in attacking a school because of the destabilizing impact it could have on the nation.

However, not all ideological attackers embrace extremist politics. They may simply be fanatical and dangerous advocates of mainstream causes. In the summer of 2017, the quiet scene of a congressional baseball practice in suburban Washington, D.C., was shattered by gunfire.

The shooter had expressed years of outrage toward the Republican Party on social media. According to CNN, he "defined himself publicly by his firm support of Bernie Sanders' progressive politics – and his hatred of conservatives and President Donald Trump."[36]

When the shooter arrived at the Alexandria, Va., baseball complex, he confirmed the Republican team was the one on the field.[37] Then, with two weapons, he opened fire, hitting Republican Rep. Steve Scalise and four others.

"The field was basically a killing field," said Sen. Ron Paul, one of the baseball team members.[38]

---

[36] CNN: "Suspect in congressional shooting was Bernie Sanders supporter, strongly anti-Trump" https://cnn.it/2GscmKE
[37] NBC: "Congressional Baseball Gunman Had List of GOP Lawmakers' Names" https://nbcnews.to/2DFGlxb
[38] The New York Times: "Congressman Steve Scalise Gravely Wounded in Alexandria Baseball Field Ambush" https://nyti.ms/2rgRxem

Why does all of this matter?

If we have the mistaken notion that our office will only be attacked by someone who unpredictably and unexplainably "snaps," we'll misunderstand our adversary and will be unprepared. Here's how being informed of each type of attacker can improve the safety of your workplace:

- **Criminals:** Understanding the danger of burglars, vandals and other intruders can prompt us to ensure our facilities are secure, alarmed and monitored. This minimizes the threat of an unexpected confrontation between criminals and employees.

- **Employees:** Training our staff to be attuned to warning signs displayed by co-workers, customers and vendors can defuse potential violence.

- **Domestic:** Although we can't manage our employees' home lives, we can provide supportive programs and a channel for them to report concerns about violence. Security and key employees can also be on alert for individuals who may be a threat.

- **Ideological:** Training can help co-workers be alert for employees displaying a fondness for extremism. In some instances, law enforcement should be informed.

Aesop is credited with the saying, "We often give our enemies the means for our own destruction."

Don't give them the keys. Instead, let's bar the door.

CHAPTER 4

The High Cost of Inaction

Preparing for a threat takes time and resources, but it's nothing compared to the real thing.

"If you think safety is expensive, try an accident."
— Trevor Kletz

It's hard to think of something more devastating for a workplace than a shooting.

Go ahead. Think about it.

What could be worse than a blood-spattered office, body bags and images that can never be unseen?

But if that's not enough, consider that workplace violence puts the survival of your business on the line. It costs companies $121 billion per year.[39] If you want to

---

[39] Includes expenses associated with lost business and productivity, litigation, medical care, psychiatric care, higher insurance rates, increased security measures, negative publicity and loss of employees. Sources: Northwestern Mutual Life Insurance Study on Workplace Violence, U.S. Department of Justice, and U.S. Department of Health and Human Services, U.S. Bureau of Labor Statistics, National Safe Workplace Institute, National Institute for Occupational Safety and Health (NIOSH), Society for Human Resource Management, Security Director News, Institute for Crisis Management, ASIS International.

improve your bottom line, not to mention the safety and morale of your employees, here's one place you can start.

Consequence #1: Liability

After a tragedy, it would be nice to have a reprieve. But litigators and regulators will give you no respite. Courts and government agencies will judge your business based on these questions:

- Could the problem (workplace violence) have been anticipated?

- If so, what did you do to prevent it?

The Las Vegas concert shooting in 2017 will forever live as a dark moment in U.S. history. But the conflict didn't end when the last shot was fired.

More than a dozen lawsuits were filed within weeks of the assault. Plaintiffs contend hotel and concert officials took inadequate measures to prevent the shooting. The legal process is expected to last years.[40]

In the judgment of courts and regulators, workplaces must be able to demonstrate they took reasonable efforts to prevent harm. "Reasonable" is the key word because it's impossible to eliminate all threats to your workplace.

---

[40] McGowan Program Administrators: "What Happens in the Aftermath of an Active Shooter Situation?" https://bit.ly/2C2oofL; Los Angeles Times: "Mandalay Bay and concert promoter sued by hundreds of Las Vegas massacre survivors" https://lat.ms/2IF6roj

(Despite world-class security, diplomats and world leaders are still assassinated.)

In legal circles, the term used to describe adequate preparation is "due diligence preparedness."

OSHA's General Duty Clause[41] requires a workplace free of "recognizable hazards." This means your business needs policies, training and an action plan to address the threat. If your office is struck by violence and you fail to demonstrate preparedness, you may be subject to staggering financial penalties. Making matters worse, evidence from an OSHA ruling could be used in civil litigation. A Massachusetts health care facility, for example, was fined more than $200,000 by OSHA.[42]

The financial and legal risks don't stop at the door of businesses. The plague of school shootings has heightened interest in mass attack coverage, according to Insurance Journal.

"School districts often find that their general liability policies fall short on coverage for the cascade of bills that follow a violent incident like the mass shooting ... in Parkland, Florida."[43]

---

[41] OSHA: "Workplace Violence" https://bit.ly/2koDQpm
[42] OSHA: "OSHA Investigation Finds Psychiatric Hospital Workers Remain Exposed to Serious Workplace Hazards" https://bit.ly/2P7GYGl
[43] Insurance Journal: "More School Districts Buying Active Shooter Insurance" https://bit.ly/2lO7bH9

Costs for schools can include litigation, facility repairs, medical expenses, counseling and specialized services such as accounting, public relations and construction.

Schools aren't the only organizations purchasing active shooter insurance. Office buildings, concert halls and other venues with exposure to mass attacks have begun seeking coverage.

After a workplace assault, it's never business as usual.

Consequence #2: The bottom line

After a workplace assault, it's never business as usual. In addition to the risk of rising insurance rates, government fines and litigation, your business may have to temporarily shut down.

And some may never reopen.

"There's been some difficult discussions with CEOs to say, 'Hey, this facility is going to be out of service ... for a week while we process the crime scene,'" according to FBI Special Agent Christopher Combs. "I think sometimes companies don't think about that and they get caught in a lurch."[44]

---

[44] Business Insurance: "Employers intensify preparation for active shooter incidents" https://bit.ly/2yct3r9

Excel Industries, the Hesston, Kan., manufacturing plant mentioned earlier in this book, closed for 11 days following an attack.

In addition[45]:

- There can be up to a 50% decrease in productivity in the 6-18 weeks following an incident.

- Employee turnover can soar to 20-40%.

- The cumulative cost of a single workplace homicide averages between $250,000 and $1 million.

- The average out-of-court settlement for a workplace violence lawsuit is nearly $500,000; the average jury award is $43 million.

- The cost of a negligence lawsuit has increased from approximately $800,000 per case in 1995 to nearly $2 million.

- Because of workplace violence, 500,000 employees miss 1.8 million days of work annually.

The 2007 attack on Virginia Tech is Exhibit A. In addition to the horrific shooting deaths of 32 people, there

---

[45] National Institute for the Prevention of Workplace Violence: "The Financial Impact of Workplace Violence" https://bit.ly/2Paer2Y; AFSCME Health & Safety Fact Sheet: "Workplace Violence" https://bit.ly/2DVHxlh

was a massive financial impact. One study calculated the cost at $48 million[46]:

- $11.4 million: Safety and security upgrades
- $6.4 million: Cleanup, renovations and other facility changes
- $4.8 million: Settlement payments and other legal costs
- $2.7 million: Support for survivors and families of victims
- $3.2 million: Other operational expenses
- $9.5 million: State expenses, including settlements
- $590,000: Healthcare costs

Even if the study was wrong by half, the figures would still be staggering.

And then there's the impact on your brand itself. It's possible your company could be associated with workplace violence for years to come. After all, where did the term "going postal" come from?

In 1986, a postal employee in Edmond, Okla., shot 20 co-workers, killing 14, before taking his own life. A series of

---

[46] The Washington Post: "Report: Virginia Tech massacre cost $48.2 million" https://wapo.st/2IDOlxp

postal employee shootings in the next few years locked the term "going postal" into the American lexicon.

Other examples of organizations tied to tragedy include:

- Sandy Hook Elementary
- Columbine High School
- Virginia Tech
- First Baptist Church of Sutherland Springs, Texas
- Pulse Nightclub (Orlando, Fla.)
- Fort Hood, Texas

Some incidents won't be remembered nationwide, but will leave a lasting impact in their hometowns. Examples include:

- A mass shooting at Excel Industries in rural Hesston, Kan., in 2016.
- A shooting at the Clovis, N.M., public library, in 2017 where a teenage assailant killed two and injured four.
- The 2006 killing of five students in a one-room Amish school in Nickel Mines, Pa.

In the Pennsylvania attack, Lancaster Online noted[47] residents are apt to use another community's name when asked where they're from.

"That's because people recognize the name of their small village and remember 'the happening' – as the families call it – that occurred there."

No matter the level of media exposure, having your brand connected with a shooting is a terrible association for employees, investors and your community.

The bottom line

The costs of recovering from an active shooter incident far outweigh the work of seeking to prevent one.

- What are the costs of doing something?
- What are the costs of doing nothing?

And what price are you willing to pay?

---

[47]Lancaster Online: "Nickel Mines, 5 Years Later: A daily walk for Amish on path of grief and forgiveness" https://bit.ly/2EHrGaF

CHAPTER 5

Prepare to Prevail

Overcoming workplace violence begins with a practical, actionable plan.

"The only thing harder than planning for an emergency is explaining why you didn't." – Anonymous

Planning is embedded in the DNA of every organization. Teachers have lesson plans. Churches plan worship services. Businesses plan for peak seasons. And everybody plans a budget.

Yet when it comes to emergencies, many of these same organizations have no plan – or at least nothing that will actually help in a crisis.

Often, when a fire alarm sounds, employees sit and look at each other with blank stares. After shrugging their shoulders, they return to work, assuming the alarm was false. But what if it was real?

This is evidence of a lack of planning.

Do you have an emergency response plan? Not one in a dusty file cabinet, but a current, active plan that employees are ready to enact?

And if so, does it include workplace violence and mass attacks?

Not only can a plan save your employees and your business, it can also provide a strong defense in the event you are sued. A plan is evidence you took the threat seriously and acted to prevent it.

Calling 911 is not a plan

Don't get us wrong: *You must call 911.* But calling the police should be only one component of a multi-faceted strategy.

Why is that?

1. The average response time between a 911 call and the arrival of police is 4-9 minutes. And that's just door-to-door. If your site has several acres or thousands of square feet, the response will take longer.

2. How long would it take for an armed assailant to wipe out your entire office? When bullets are flying, four minutes is an eternity.

If you still think law enforcement can completely protect your workplace, consider the Virginia Tech shooting in 2007. Police responded in record time – two minutes. But despite their speed, 32 people died in the attack.

Law enforcement plays a critical role. The better they know you and your facility, the more effective they can be in a crisis. *But you must have your own strategy to prevail until police arrive.*

The details are important

Often employers answer "yes" when asked if they have a workplace violence program. But upon further inspection, the plan often consists of a singular policy of no tolerance toward bullying and harassment. Although this is necessary, it's only one piece of a much larger puzzle.

What should a program include?

- A comprehensive policy
- A document stating its intended purpose
- A policy for reporting and responding to domestic violence
- A high-risk termination policy
- An intruder response action plan
- Employee perception assessments
- Educational materials on (1) personal conduct to minimize violence (2) warning signs of workplace violence

Let's get into the details.

#1 Your policy

This outlines what you will and won't tolerate in the workplace when it comes to violence, threats and aggressive behavior. It gives you an authoritative standard to use when dealing with aggression. It also establishes protocol for reporting incidents and getting help and support to employees facing crises. The goal of a policy is to weed out the bad apples of workplace violence before they rot and contaminate.

#2 Threat assessment

When it comes to security vulnerabilities, every business is unique. Risks could include your customers, employees or the nature of your facility (see chapter 2). A truly useful assessment will determine what threats are relevant to your organization and avoids generic approaches.

You must avoid a cookie-cutter strategy.

That means you must avoid a cookie-cutter strategy. This is usually a collection of other organizations' crisis plans cut and pasted off the internet. These approaches don't work for other parts of your business and they certainly won't stop an active threat.

Because a generic plan takes no inventory of your organization's risks, it may be a solution in search of a problem. Or it may completely miss serious vulnerabilities to your security.

If your organization has a plan, it can't be one that was created years ago and is collecting dust. It must be active, updated and understood by everyone involved.

Who should conduct the assessment?

While even a limited risk assessment is better than nothing, businesses should consider getting an outsider's perspective.

You could conduct your own assessment, but this approach is limited by the facts that:

- You don't know what you don't know.

- Unless you're a security consultant, you're at best an amateur when it comes to assessing vulnerabilities.

- It's difficult to be objective about your own organization.

- A professional assessment and plan is more likely to withstand legal scrutiny than a DIY version.

In addition, your insurer may offer discounts for having a professional crisis response plan.

Unless you have the specific skill set required, it's highly unlikely you would try to replace your own vehicle's transmission, mud jack your home's foundation or undertake complex business tax preparations that will be reviewed by the IRS. The well-being of your people is far more important than any of those things.

If you fail to accurately assess the threat, the results could be devastating. That's why we recommend using a trustworthy consulting company instead of trying to "hack" your security.

#3 Your response to the threat assessment

What weaknesses did your assessment reveal? Now it's time to address them. The most effective response is layered. That means if an assailant gets in the front door, you have additional barriers in place to stop him. Options

It's not enough to be reactive and merely discipline an employee after the fact. The goal is to educate, prevent and defuse aggression before it starts.

include cameras, locks, swipe cards and security guards. A professional consultant can help you decide which options are most important for your organization. Because budgets are finite, you can determine top priorities and phase in security improvements incrementally.

#4 Incident management

When it comes to addressing workplace violence at your organization, someone needs to own it. Who will be tasked with responding to threats and violations of policy?

It's not enough to be reactive and merely discipline an employee after the fact. The goal is to educate, prevent and defuse aggression before it starts. The task of addressing workplace violence must be proactive and ongoing.

#5 Training

In order for your plan to be more than a paper tiger, training must be scheduled and repeated. Education should equip employees and managers to:

- Recognize behavioral warning signs of workplace violence and report concerns.

- Understand where they can get help for managing stress at home or work.

- Manage a high-risk termination.

- Respond effectively in a crisis.

Training is not a one-time event. It must be continuous. Repetition is the key to success. Practicing your plan will also reveal occasional changes you need to make.

Rehearsing a plan helps employees learn to work through a crisis even when they feel overwhelmed. Instead of reacting instinctively, they'll take productive action.

A good rule of thumb is to train employees every six months and any time there are major changes to the plan. In addition, employees should be periodically tested on their knowledge through supervised drills and refresher training. Even the best strategy is only as good as your workers' ability to carry it out.

Speak no evil?

Employers may be tempted to "see no evil, hear no evil, speak no evil" when it comes to workplace violence. Out of a concern of stirring fear, they may say nothing. This, in fact, has the opposite effect. Employees who are trained are more at ease, less anxious and more confident.

Fear is the result of having a problem with no solution. Once you educate employees to respond, fear and anxiety recede. They appreciate management taking the lead instead of putting its head in the sand.

Assessing + planning + training = Prevailing

CHAPTER 6

Nobody "Just Snaps"
Understanding people and patterns is the key to countering workplace violence.

"Have we become observationally lazy? Have we allowed ourselves to become careless when it comes to our own safety and that of our loved ones?"
– Joe Navarro

Pens and paper. Budgets. Meeting room 369R. It started out as another uneventful faculty meeting at the University of Alabama in Huntsville.

But, as Wired magazine reported, things were about to change. One of the professors in the room had a Ruger 9-mm semiautomatic pistol. And plans to use it.

"For the better part of an hour, [Professor Amy] Bishop had been sitting at the end of a long conference table, listening to a dozen people discuss the biology department's budget and other matters. Now standing near the room's only door, she was transformed. Aiming at one colleague's head after another, she pulled the trigger again and again. Boom. Boom.

"With six people wounded, there was blood everywhere – on the table, on the chairs, on the white drywall.

Someone used a coffee table to barricade the door. Someone else found a cell phone and dialed 911."[48]

Three were dead. And there would have been more, but a gun malfunction stopped the rampage. Bishop headed to the building's loading dock and phoned her husband to pick her up.

"I'm done," she told him.

The Harvard-trained neurobiologist was sentenced to life in prison.[49]

Wired magazine began an extensive report on Bishop by asking, "What makes a smart, well-educated mother of four go on a killing spree?"

A closer look revealed that, behind Bishop's professorial manner, lay decades of violent and aggressive behavior.[50]

Indicators

It's rare an employee experiences a 180-degree change in personality and suddenly becomes violent. Instead, investigations routinely reveal a pattern of behavioral

---

[48] Wired: "What Made This University Researcher Snap?" https://bit.ly/2yQU0C0

[49] NBC News: "After Five Years, Alabama Killer Apologizes for the First Time" https://nbcnews.to/2D6TxOP

[50] Wired: "What Made This University Researcher Snap?" https://bit.ly/2yQU0C0

problems that may or may not have been known to management. *Yet the warning signs are there.*

A recent FBI report concluded: "The commonly held perception that mass shooters are mostly mentally ill people who brood in silence and give few warning signs is incorrect and could hamper efforts to identify attackers before they kill."[51]

The ability to identify risk indicators could mean life or death in the workplace.

If it sounds like the ability to identify risk indicators could mean life or death, you're correct.

Give me a sign

What, then, are the warning signs? While there is no comprehensive list – and human intuition is required – indicators include:

- Veiled or direct threats.

- A recent fascination with weapons.

- Claims of being victimized or persecuted.

- Recent and significant changes in moods, attitudes and behaviors.

---

[51] Los Angeles Times: "Parkland school shooter: Typical of today's mass killers studied by FBI" https://lat.ms/2OO6RyX

- Excessive absenteeism.

- Boundary probing and escalation.

- Aggravation related to finances, relationships or the workplace.

- Failure to accept responsibility.

- Diagnosed or demonstrated mental health issues.

Body language

Psychologists agree that non-verbal behavior and tone of voice are key components of communication. In fact, they reveal more than the actual words spoken by an individual.

If we focus only on verbal content, we may miss a threat staring us in the face. When a person pounds a fist against a file cabinet, it tells us much more about his state of mind than when he says, "This is a lousy day."

Because of the disproportionate importance of body language, team members need to be trained in observing and interpreting non-verbal behavior – especially actions that are out of the ordinary.

In our training, we use the acronym JDLR to illustrate this point. JDLR stands for "Just Doesn't Look Right." It has nothing to do with age, ethnicity, religion or gender. It has everything to do with the person's general countenance, an awkward manner of dress (that might be concealing a weapon) and his level of social engagement.

All of us have a God-given "Spidey sense" about these things. The question is: Are we going to acknowledge it or ignore it?

We don't want to judge a book by its cover, but we need to be aware of JDLR indicators. We must avoid the extremes of both paranoia and obliviousness. Instead, listen to your internal Spidey.

"Keep your friends close but your enemies closer."
– Michael Corleone, "The Godfather"

You see unusual behavior: Now what?
While we may be tempted to keep JDLR individuals at a distance, that's the opposite of what a safety-conscious employee should do.

As that famous security expert Michael Corleone said in "The Godfather": "Keep your friends close but your enemies closer."

This doesn't mean having spies hide behind plants in the lobby, clicking pictures with cell phones. Rather, it means communicating, talking and listening to people with JDLR indicators.

If someone seems out of sorts, give him a warm greeting and make eye contact. If the person is disoriented or struggling emotionally, you may be able to offer genuine help. If he is someone intending harm, he'll immediately know others have noticed him and may abandon his plan. This is similar to deterring shoplifters: If they you're watching, they leave.

Engaging may also interrupt someone planning self-harm – a phenomenon that has engulfed the workplace. The Bureau of Labor statistics reported 291 workplace suicides in 2016 – the most recorded since record keeping began in 1992.[52]

On the church security detail where Vaughn Baker (one of the authors) serves in the Kansas City area, his team noticed a JDLR individual. They were convinced he meant others no harm, but were still concerned about his condition. Security asked a pastor to follow up with this man before he left the building that morning.

Later Vaughn learned the man was planning to kill himself after the worship service. The security team's awareness and the pastor's caring intervention saved a life. This kind of observant approach isn't limited to houses of worship. A little bit of awareness can go a long way in protecting employees from self-harm.

Characteristics of an aware employee
Instead of shrugging their shoulders and turning their

---

[52] Bureau of Labor Statistics: "Census of Fatal Occupational Injuries Summary, 2016" https://bit.ly/2iuZZ8g

backs on people who seem odd, engaged employees speak up and take action. By being proactive, many violent confrontations can be defused.

This is the art of awareness.

There's a popular satirical routine on TV where a customer approaches an employee for help. The common refrain is, "I don't know nuthin', I just work here." This is the antitheses of an aware employee. Instead of being oblivious, alert employees notice:

- When an employee hasn't showed up for work or has frequent absences.

- When a colleague seems depressed or disgruntled.

- When a coworker mentions fear of a spouse or domestic partner.

In addition, alert and trained employees will identify people who don't belong on your property. If name badges are required, an educated worker will speak up when someone lacks ID.

If your protocol requires guests to buzz in and visually confirm their identity, a trained employee will refuse entry to strangers. Ditto for holding the door open for people without ID. Instead, employees should ask the guest, "How can I help you today?" and then direct them to the security desk.

If there is no warning and an aggressor enters the building in a burst of violence, then it's time for emergency measures. We'll introduce *The Three Out Response Model* in Chapter 10.

But before we do, remember this: You win 100 percent of the battles you never fight.

Be alert. Recognize suspicious behavior. Defuse it whenever possible.

CHAPTER 7

High-risk Terminations and Interactions

Parting ways is never easy, but it doesn't have to be deadly.

"Better a thousand times careful than once dead."
– Proverb

Nancy Swift was a beloved nurse in Mississippi and Alabama for 40 years. She survived two battles with cancer but ultimately succumbed to gunshots following an employee reprimand.

When the 63-year-old nurse confronted a staff member at UAB Highlands in Birmingham, he shot Swift and another employee before killing himself.[53]

"It was an employee relations issue that led to what happened," said Lt. Peter Williston of the Birmingham Police Department.[54]

There's no such thing as a pleasant termination or reprimand. But sometimes it rises to the level of a security

---

[53] AL.com: "Funerals set for UAB Highlands nurse killed in workplace shooting" https://bit.ly/2OsUTFM
[54] U.S. News & World Report: "Police: Disgruntled Worker Killed Nurse in Alabama Hospital" https://bit.ly/2PG0m0x

risk. In that event, not only is the supervisor in danger: A violent incident could put all your employees' safety on the line.

How do you know when a termination is risky? There are two patterns of behavior to be aware of.

#1 Overtly aggressive personnel
These employees stand out. It doesn't take a trained specialist to identify the problem. Employees like this are being terminated for making threats, being rude and intimidating the workplace. They've already demonstrated they're dangerous. You'd be crazy not to treat this termination with extra care.

The passive aggressive employee can be as great a threat as the overtly hostile worker.

#2 The ticking time bomb
The passive aggressive employee can be as great a threat as the overtly hostile worker. The problem is, his symptoms can easily go unnoticed.

While this worker is not disruptive, his performance is on a steadily downward trajectory.

Why is this a high-risk termination?

An out-of-character decline in performance can indicate a serious personal crisis with roots outside the workplace.

This employee is an explosive device waiting to be triggered. Violence usually escalates through a process, not an isolated event. If you are terminating someone displaying these characteristics, it may be wise to involve a behavior assessment specialist. (This is an area of Strategos' expertise. Please contact us if we can be of assistance.)

High-risk termination factors

Does a termination pose cause for concern? Here are a few profiles of individuals and indicators to be aware of.

#1 Personal stress

Mason is a quiet but serious presence at the machine shop. But outside the office, his personal life is on the rocks. His wife just issued a restraining order against him and they're separated for the second time. On his breaks, it's common for phone calls to his wife to degenerate into shouting matches. It's natural for someone to seek reconciliation with a spouse, but for Mason it's become an obsession.

#2 The loner

Emma always eats lunch by herself and avoids work-related social functions. What she lacks in friends, she makes up for in an obsessive focus on her job. It appears to have become her sole identity and purpose in life.

#3 Weapons obsession

Michael was never a "gun guy." Hunting and target shooting weren't his thing. But in his mid-30s that changed. Guns became a daily topic of conversation at work, even with people who had no interest. He seemed to relish posting pictures of guns, and himself holding weapons, on social media. One, seen by several colleagues, featured him elatedly shooting a handgun into the ground again and again.

#4 Threatening and unfiltered

Benjamin issues threats so regularly that people have stopped taking him seriously. "That's just Ben." But collectively, his direct and veiled threats in and outside the workplace add up. Sometimes they materialize. Although he denied involvement, tires were slashed in the parking lot after a heated conflict with a co-worker. Workspaces were anonymously vandalized. In addition to his aggression, Benjamin routinely uses offensive language when discussing women and minorities.

#5 Blaming others

For Sophia, it's always someone else's fault. When she misses a deadline, it's because the programmers didn't get their part done early enough. When she's late for work, it's the "idiots on the road." When her work is riddled with errors, it's because she works in an "oppressive environment."

#6 The ideologue

There's no question where you'll find Elijah on his lunch hour. He'll be in the break room on his phone, lighting up social media and message boards with rants about government surveillance. "You know they're listening to you right now, don't you?" he tells those trying eat in peace. Elijah has been reprimanded multiple times for engaging in anti-surveillance activism on company time.

These six profiles do not represent a comprehensive list. Employers concerned about a volatile termination are advised to get professional help to avoid a worst-case scenario. Better safe than sorry.

The keys to defusing a potentially risky termination are planning, training and consulting. Because the stakes are high, leave nothing to chance.

High-risk terminations 101
When any task is considered high-risk, we leave it to people who are trained and experienced. A potentially problematic termination is not a training opportunity for a new manager or something to be blindly delegated. Why? There are too many critical factors that can be easily overlooked, including time of day, day of week and even the room where termination takes place. Experience proves these things matter.

Nor, under any circumstances, should a high-risk termination be relegated to a manager who is sick of the employee's poor performance and wants to "stick it to him."

The keys to defusing a potentially risky termination are planning, training and consulting. Because the stakes are high, leave nothing to chance.

A supervisor at Benada Aluminum Products in Sanford, Fla., learned about the stakes first hand. Police say a terminated worker waited in ambush to kill his boss just two hours after being let go. The ex-employee unleashed a barrage of gunfire and chased the supervisor for more than a mile before giving up the pursuit. He was charged with attempted homicide.[55]

As anyone who has terminated an employee knows, it's a highly-charged event under the best of circumstances. When warning signs arise, caution is mandatory.

Unpacking a high-risk termination

They'd given him every chance to succeed, but Collin seemed firmly fixed on a path of disruption.

The software programmer routinely argued with his manager and seemed to delight in publicly showing up his co-workers. In his mind, he was always the smartest person in the room.

---

[55] KSBW 8: "Man hired and fired within 3 days admits to shooting at boss, police say" https://bit.ly/2A2WRJ6; New York Daily News "Office employee tries to kill boss hours after he's terminated" https://nydn.us/2CaEzXY

Despite Collin's tech savvy, his managers didn't let his misbehavior go unchallenged. His personnel file included three reprimands and a 90-day probation. He was on day 33 when the company decided he had to go.

Things came to a head when Collin exploded at the director of finance during a conversation about malfunctioning software.

Supervisors concluded there was no way the business could function effectively with a loose cannon running amok.

Collin's manager, Kaitlin, knew this termination had warning signs written all over it. She'd watched too many dire news reports to simply wing it. So she spoke with HR, senior leadership and a security consultant before sitting down for the termination.

As a result, Kaitlin took pains to plan every detail of the meeting. She chose a private location to spare Collin humiliation. But she deliberately chose a room with an outside exit.

Why?

Having immediate access to the parking lot would allow Collin to save face by simply walking out to his car. There would be no box-in-hand parade through the building. But the quick exit also served another purpose: If things got out of control, Kaitlin could flee.

She also recognized the wisdom of having a third person in the room. Eric, the operations manager, could vouch for anything that was or wasn't said during the meeting. He could also serve as a defender if the meeting turned violent.

Kaitlin studied the layout of the room. She re-arranged the open space and put a desk between herself and Collin. She, not Collin, would be nearest the exit.

Kaitlin was also ready to communicate clear expectations. Collin was to leave immediately. His personal belongings would be collected and delivered to him. His final paycheck would also be in hand. And, under no circumstances could he re-enter the building.

Human resources and IT were confidentially informed Collin would be leaving on a specified date and time. At 10 a.m., they were to revoke all of his clearances and computer network access. His credit card would be canceled and his photo would be given to reception and security personnel with the instructions, "Deny access."

Flipping the switch

At 9:55 a.m., Kaitlin summoned Eric, swallowed the lump in her throat and asked Collin to the meeting room. She kept the conversation cordial but to the point, handing him a folder with his paycheck and information on benefits and outplacement assistance.

Collin, for once, was speechless. He looked down, shook his head, shrugged his shoulders and walked out the door to the parking lot.

As anyone who has terminated an employee knows, it's a highly-charged event under the best of circumstances. When warning signs arise, caution is mandatory.

The locked door gently clicked behind him.

Kaitlin, however, was taking no chances. She received approval to have a security presence on the premises for the remainder of the day and the following week. In addition, she advised the reception team, human resources and company leadership to be alert.

The same meeting could have been handled differently – and with catastrophic results. If Kaitlin allowed the conversation to degenerate into an argument, anger could have spiraled out of control. If Collin was humiliated in front of his colleagues, he might have sought revenge.

This, of course, was a fictional narrative. But it provides many of the facts you need to turn a potential worst-case scenario into a merely unpleasant meeting.

Create a soft landing

Although you can't take the sting out of a termination, you can take several actions to soften the blow and reduce the chances of a flare-up:

- **Consult with a high-risk termination specialist.** An outside expert can investigate the circumstances and make a recommendation. In addition, the consultant can tell the employee that termination is recommended and, as a result, the company has no choice. This can take the target off the employer and redirect it toward the consultant.

- **Provide employment assistance services.** Your human resources team can help the employee find a new job.

- **Offer a severance package.** It may be appropriate to offer severance in exchange for a resignation. This avoids an official termination, allows the employee to save face and can defuse anger.

After the separation

If you've had to release an employee, you understand both the feelings of regret and relief when the task is complete. But is it done?

With a high-risk termination, the answer is no.

In the real-life example we shared earlier in this chapter, an ex-employee was charged with ambushing his supervisor two hours after termination. But revenge isn't always immediate. Be observant of anniversaries surrounding the employee's hiring or release date and take appropriate precautions.

In addition, we recommend a heightened security approach for two weeks following a high-risk termination.

Although we can't live in a bubble, we caution at-risk managers and employees to be aware of their surroundings. Security teams and gatekeepers must remain vigilant at all times.

Unfortunately, the risk of aggression does not end at the workplace door. Any emotionally-charged separation or decision can result in unintended consequences.

Beyond the workplace: other high-risk encounters
Unfortunately, the risk of aggression does not end at the workplace door. Any emotionally-charged separation or decision can result in unintended consequences.

In Federal Way, Wash., Charles and Carol Parsons attended a counseling session at Calvary Lutheran Church. When Carol said she would not reconcile, Charles pulled a pistol from his jacket and pointed it at the counselor. Then he turned to his wife and shot her six times.[56]

Charles called 911 and got right to the point: "I just flew into a massive fit of rage and shot my wife during counseling."

Forewarned is forearmed. In our rage-filled age, be on high-alert in the following circumstances:

- Revoking someone's church or organizational membership.

- Expelling a student.

- Barring someone from entering your facility.

- Any entanglement in a divorce or relational breakup.

If it's emotionally charged, be prepared. Don't gamble with high-risk terminations or separations of any kind.

When it comes to workplace violence, unlike casinos, the house doesn't always win.

---

[56] KOMO: "28-year sentence for man who killed wife during counseling session" https://bit.ly/2yyZD7M

CHAPTER 8

Secure Your Facility

Make it difficult for someone to storm the gates.

"Little pig, little pig, let me come in."
"Not by the hair on my chiny chin chin."
– The Three Little Pigs

With our nation's high level of anxiety about school shootings, you'd expect every school to be difficult for outsiders to enter. Unfortunately, this is not the case. An investigative report by a Missouri newspaper tested an urban school district's defenses and found them lacking.

At two public high schools, the reporter simply pressed the button on a call box and was allowed to enter, no questions asked. Once inside, she was able to wander the halls freely. At the third school, a student held the door for her and allowed her in with no questions. When confronted about the lapse, a school district administrator said its policy was violated.

"That's not the protocol."[57]

Although we appreciate that rules were in place, the same result would have occurred had there been none.

---

[57] St. Joseph, Mo., News-Press Now: "School safety starts at the front door" https://bit.ly/2P06VLn

This free-for-all admittance policy is not only an issue for schools. It's frequent in businesses, church offices and day care centers.

If anyone can walk in, then anything can happen.

As we discussed in Chapter 2, some businesses don't have the option of screening visitors and locking doors. Hospitals and retailers are two examples.

But let's start with the low-hanging fruit. If you can lock your door and screen visitors, do it. It can save lives.

However, we don't want to overstate the risk of outside threats. Most attacks come from inside. In schools, 82 percent of incidents come from within. Bullet-resistant windows and high-tech surveillance offer no protection from this type of attacker.

But what about metal detectors? First of all, they are labor intensive and require multiple personnel to operate correctly. In addition, a serious attacker will move his assault to a foyer, playground or parking lot – vulnerable areas unscreened by detectors.

Think layers

If an attacker is committed, he can get through nearly any security barrier.

So why try?

Barriers are not intended to be impenetrable. Rather, they are impediments and obstacles. And some barriers will completely dissuade an attacker.

When a school shooter encounters a locked door, he often moves on to another, softer target. Even if he chooses to shoot the door open, he's burning time and bullets.

And consider this: Before the shooter got to a classroom door, he had to overcome barriers at the front door. Both obstacles slowed him down and gave the faculty and police time to respond.

As we teach at Strategos International: *Lock, layer and reinforce.*

Beyond the front door

Security begins before an attacker gets to the entrance.

Even bad guys have to park. If you have eyes and ears in parking lots and garages, you're ahead of the game.

Trained and aware team members recognize strange body language and unusual attire in parking areas. If someone is carrying large duffel bags and looks nervous, something may be up. Better to alert security than to be sorry.

The Sutherland Springs, Texas, church attacker walked across a street and through the parking lot in broad daylight. He wore black tactical clothing with a clearly visible weapon. Yet no one saw him coming. Parking attendants may have been able to initiate lockdown.

Dark, empty parking areas and garages are frequent crime scenes. Burglaries, auto thefts, assaults and homicides can and do happen in these unguarded acres. Keep the lights on and security measures, such as cameras, visible.

If there is a concern, have security escort workers to their cars after dark. If you have no security, encourage employees to leave in pairs. Even if it's a bright and sunny day, workers need to be alert. They should have their keys in hand, put down their phones and pay attention.

If you can restrict access to your building, do so. That may mean locking a door or only admitting employees with swipe cards. All others must get approval from security.

Building access

If you can restrict access to your building, do so. That may mean locking a door or only admitting employees with swipe cards. All others must get approval from security.

Well-meaning workers may see holding the door for strangers as a friendly gesture. They need to be instructed otherwise: No card, no entrance.

Visitors to the workplace must be clearly designated with a guest tag. Alert employees will spot people who lack credentials and ask if they need assistance.

Security cameras can have a deterring effect and also document criminal acts. However, if someone is bent on destruction, he probably won't mind if the last minutes of his life are caught on video. On the other hand, cameras monitored in real time can alert security to suspicious activity.

In addition to requiring access and permission to enter front doors, duplicating this process in multiple areas of a building adds still more layers of security. This approach is effective for locations including schools and hospitals. Hospitals, for example, can restrict guests to the floor of the patient they are visiting by using color-coded passes.

Trained employees are prepared to recognize someone in an unauthorized area, redirect them and notify security. This approach reduces access to potential victims. Although some may object that it's inconvenient, it's much less cumbersome than being shot. Security and convenience do not go hand-in-hand. It's a consultant's job to help employers find the right balance.

Lock. Layer. Reinforce.

Evaluating your facility
The best time to consider facility security is when you're building or expanding a workplace.

Security professionals can work with an architect to maximize safety without compromising building aesthetics, functionality or brand identity.

Unfortunately, security is often last on the list of considerations, whether it's a factory or a school. Building plans are approved by fire officials, construction code inspectors and environmental regulators. But nothing is required from a security perspective. Given our violent world, security should be the first priority.

If you're stuck with an existing building that isn't optimized for security, improvements can still be made. These may include the addition of a safe room, locks and cameras.

We encourage any workplace serious about safety to commission a physical security audit. You don't know what you don't know. Many times a series of small improvements can make a big difference.

As important as this is, there's something even more important. In fact, it's your greatest security asset. We'll explore it in the next chapter.

CHAPTER 9
Security Rises and Falls on Employee Training
Equip your team to prevail over raw instincts and fear.

"We don't rise to the level of our expectations. We fall to the level of our training." — Archilochus

Lisa and Chad Remley thought they were going to a concert. Instead, they ended up in a kill zone.

They had the misfortune of attending the Route 91 Harvest Festival in Las Vegas in 2017. That's the event where a gunman fired more than 1,000 bullets into a massive crowd, killing 58 and injuring hundreds more.

But the Missouri couple had an advantage: Training. And they say it saved their lives.

"I feel lucky that I took the training beforehand," said Chad. "It was almost automatic that it went in to play."

"I said, 'I'm scared,'" recalled Lisa. "He said, 'Don't be scared. ... You just have to trust me.'"[58]

---

[58] KSDK TV, St. Louis: "Local couple says active shooter training saved them in Las Vegas" https://on.ksdk.com/2APSUrH

Since even the best physical security can be breached, alert personnel are the first line of defense.

In Chapter 8, we explained ways to harden your facility and keep out unwanted "guests." While this is essential, it's not *the* most important thing you can do.

Well, what is it then?

Your No. 1 priority is training employees.

Since even the best physical security can be breached, alert personnel are the first line of defense.

In addition, the vast majority of threats come from within. No amount of facility hardening will stop them. What about the disgruntled employee who arrives with a backpack full of guns and ammunition? He has a swipe card and an ID badge. Only an aware team member stands between him and an office massacre.

The difference training makes
We can't overstate the power of training. It turns timid targets into people of productive action.

This is true not only in the realm of active shooter response. Training brings confidence across disciplines of all sorts. However, the extreme duress of an attack makes education and practice all the more crucial.

Workplace violence is a topic loaded with fear. Because of this, many employers make the mistake of not discussing it. Yet employees' fears are heightened when there is no discussion or plan. Their anxieties are alleviated when they know their employer is proactive and looking out for their best interests.

Trained vs. untrained responses
Based on our own experience and analyzing the data from numerous incidents, we've identified two clear patterns when attacks occur.

The untrained response:

- Denial and disbelief

- Panic

- Helplessness

The trained response:

- Acceptance of the crisis

- Awareness

- Recall of training that leads to responsiveness and action

Responding vs. reacting
When we have an unanticipated response to medication,

we call it a reaction. No one wants that outcome. Instead, we want our body to *respond* to the medication.

This mirrors our goal in responding to a workplace assault. Our natural, instinctual *reaction* will almost always be counterproductive. Training, however, allows us to overcome our instincts and prevail in a high-stress situation.

What are some of these natural reactions?

When we are threatened, a common behavior is assuming a fetal position under a desk or table or even in an open area. During the Las Vegas concert shooting, many people crouched motionless on the ground as bullets rained down upon them. It's much easier to hit an unmoving target than one in motion.

When we hear gunfire, we do not need to visually confirm its source. Getting close enough to see someone shooting will likely end your life.

Another failure of instinct is the drive to obtain visual confirmation of a threat. This is natural because 80 percent of our decision-making input is based on sight. But when we hear gunfire, we do not need to visually confirm its source. Getting close enough to see someone shooting will likely end your life.

Rationalization is another natural reaction that can lead us astray in a crisis. Our brain likes patterns to be routine, predictable and non-threatening. When disruptive events occur, we often fall prey to a psychological state known as normalcy bias.

This bias causes us to irrationally dismiss overt threats and real danger. We concoct bizarre interpretations of reality such as dismissing gunshots as cars backfiring.

We may interpret a fistfight or man waving a weapon as part of a theatrical drama when such an idea is completely out of context. Others have been hit by gunfire but disbelieved it was happening.

Of course this sounds ridiculous when we're not under pressure. But in the heat of the moment, normalcy bias is often our default mode.

The good news: We can overcome it if we are aware and trained in an alternative response.

Training trumps instinct

The purpose of crisis training is to re-orient our instinctual reactions into productive responses.

Education replaces our raw impulses with a foundation of training and experience that breaks us out of paralysis and leads to action.

Training is not merely classroom instruction. It also includes demonstrations and realistic simulations of active threats.

Hands-on training creates what is called stress inoculation. Inoculation with a vaccine introduces a biological organism that results in immunity. Introducing stress in a training environment provides the mental and behavioral stimulus to help students prevail over a genuine threat.

Scenario-based training activates the body's sympathetic nervous system – often referred to as our "fight or flight" reaction. It focuses all of our bodily responses to address the threat. Blood pressure increases, our heart rate speeds up and digestion slows.

Active learning helps people get used to operating under stress so they can make sound decisions.

Active learning helps people get used to operating under stress so they can make sound decisions. This is similar to the process muscle fibers undergo during weight training. Muscles are stressed, stretched, torn, rebuilt and strengthened. Stress inoculation stretches and strengthens our psychological, emotional and physical responses under duress.

Although the content of the training varies, this is the same approach used to educate law enforcement and military personnel.

The alternative to stress inoculation is a complete and total psychological and physical shutdown. This response is triggered by the parasympathetic nervous system, often referred to as the "rest and digest" system. Instead of ramping the body up, it shuts it down and leads to feelings of helplessness and despair. People overcome by this reaction may assume a fetal position and lose control of their bodily functions, even their bowels.

Fortunately, there is an alternative.

At Strategos, we often encounter people who are leery of participating in simulation-based training. However, in almost every instance, these same personnel finish the experience feeling victorious and energized. They no longer feel helpless.

Here's what a teacher in Sedalia, Mo., had to say: "I was very nervous about how the topic would be presented and I did not want to participate in the simulated intruder scenarios. However, today I am really glad I did. I left feeling empowered and grateful about what I learned. It was one of the best professional development trainings I have ever attended."

A Kansas City area teacher expressed similar sentiment. But her words were based on a real-life experience. After committing a homicide in the parking lot, an attacker tried to enter the school. He was thwarted.

"I am grateful for your training today," the teacher told us. "We very quickly did exactly what you trained us to do. There is no doubt that a calm and empowered staff equals less fearful students."

That's the difference training makes.

CHAPTER 10
Lock Out, Get Out, Take Out
Here's what to do when the threat is live.

"If you can't go back to your mother's womb, you'd better learn to be a good fighter." – Anchee Min

It was a sleepy Sunday morning at Burnette Chapel Church of Christ in Antioch, Tenn. But the silence was shattered when an estranged member of the congregation opened fire on churchgoers in the parking lot.

After killing one person, he entered the church with two handguns and shot six more.

The death toll may have mounted if it were not for 22-year-old Robert Engle. He battled the shooter and, in the struggle, the assailant shot himself. Engle then retrieved his own weapon from his car and held the killer at gunpoint until police arrived.

"He's the hero," Metro Nashville Police Chief Steve Anderson told The Nashville Tennessean. "He's the person who stopped this madness."[59]

---

[59] The Nashville Tennessean (2017): "Nashville churchgoer, called a 'hero' for stopping shooting, asks for prayers for victims, shooter" https://bit.ly/2Ou4TDz

At the end of the day, all of us want the madness to end. But are we willing to be a part of the solution?

When bad guys break through

In spite of our best efforts to lock, layer, reinforce and train our employees, the day may come when an active shooter invades our workplace.

Since even the president of the United States is vulnerable, you and I must be prepared to prevail under pressure.

As we've stated, we can do a great deal to thwart attackers. But there is no ironclad solution to stop them all. Despite resolute security, in 2014 a knife-carrying intruder jumped the White House fence, burst through the front door and made it near the Obama presidential living quarters before being tackled. In 2017, another intruder made it over the fence and onto the Trump White House grounds before being stopped.[60]

More infamously, President Ronald Reagan was shot in Washington, D.C., in 1981 as he left a speaking engagement flanked by the U.S. Secret Service.

---

[60] Washington Post, "White House fence-jumper made it far deeper into building than previously known" https://wapo.st/2pY2UbT; The Guardian, "Man who jumped White House fence arrested by US secret service" https://bit.ly/2pXY8v2

Since even the president of the United States is vulnerable, you and I must be prepared to prevail under pressure.

Run, hide and fight?

Have you heard the term "run, hide, fight?" It's commonly taught by federal agencies and law enforcement and has weaved its way into most news reports about active shooters. This approach was originally created as a response for an individual adult in a workplace. It was not designed, for example, for a teacher making decisions for dozens of students.

First off, we're thankful people are being trained. Some training is better than none.

However, we have reservations about the "run, hide, fight" approach. When lives are on the line, precision and clarity are critical. Words have consequences. With inadequate training, the exhortation to "run, hide, fight" leaves itself open to serious misunderstandings.

Although individual trainers may offer illuminating details, these are often lost in translation or the brevity of media reports.

Let's start with "run." This can easily conjure up the idea of rushing anywhere and everywhere. If someone simply starts running, they could flee toward the gunman and not away from him. "Run" – when used with no context – also conjures up the idea of defensive behavior

95

and victim-based reaction. Although running may be the best decision, it must be guided by a clear head – not panic.

Mark Warren (one of the authors) recently learned of a training for school personnel conducted by police. School administrators requested that officers fire blanks during the simulation. They shot 14 times throughout the building. Afterward, officers learned that no one heard all the shots. Many heard only a few. School staff, and even some of the officers, said it was difficult to tell where the sound came from. This illustrates the danger of running from an unseen gunman.

Then comes the loaded term "hide." It's another defensive word that can lead people to unwittingly become victims. For many, this may mean crouching under a table in the fetal position. As we mentioned in Chapter 9, this immobilized position often turns people into sitting ducks.

Hiding is a legitimate concept, but employees must be taught *how* and *where* to take cover. Otherwise our hiding can be compared to a preschool game of hide-and-seek. Any "hiding" should take place behind a locked, barricaded door. In a crisis, we revert to our training. If that consists of childhood games, we're in trouble.

Finally, we come to the term "fight." This concept is sometimes taught as a last resort and as the least desirable of all three options. In other words, if you cannot run or hide, then fight. This approach can create hesitation, reluctance and a sense of guilt that can minimize the effectiveness of any type of fighting response.

In reality, "fight" calls people to transition from the mindset of victim to victor, from defensive to offensive. You don't want to merely survive a workplace attack: You want to prevail. This is not a call to vigilantism or reckless behavior. Instead, a prevailing mindset is required to counter the extreme duress people experience in an attack.

"Where there is only a choice between cowardice and violence, I would advise violence."
– Gandhi

No one wants to fight. We certainly don't. But if our lives – or the lives of those entrusted to us – are at risk, what choice do we have?

Even Gandhi, the standard-bearer of non-violence, understood this and said, "Where there is only a choice between cowardice and violence, I would advise violence."

"Run, hide, fight" can be misunderstood as a pre-scripted sequence of events. In other words:

1. Try to run away from the threat.

2. If you can't run away, then hide.

3. If you are found when hiding, then fight (if you haven't been shot yet).

However, mass attacks do not give us the luxury of methodically checking off options. Sometimes fighting is the first and only response we have. At other times, we can lock the intruder out immediately. The sequence of actions should depend on the circumstances, not a scripted formula.

We want to be clear that "run, hide, fight" – properly taught and understood – can be a sound approach. However, our concerns over improper instruction and distorted understanding prompt us to opt for another approach.

A case in point occurred at Ohio State University in 2016. An attacker ran over pedestrians with his car, then attacked them with a butcher knife. When a "run, hide, fight" notification went out, students and faculty fled secure facilities and ran toward the threat.[61]

---

[61] NPR: "Suspect Killed After Knife and Vehicle Attack At Ohio State University" https://n.pr/2RCyVSS

Another common intruder response methodology is called A.L.I.C.E. This is a program from the A.L.I.C.E. Training Institute and is an acronym:

A - Alert

L - Lockdown

I - Inform

C - Counter

E - Evacuate

A.L.I.C.E. is a valid approach and contains many valuable insights to overcome an active shooter attack. Our main concern, however, is that there are too many points to remember under stress. The "rule of three" is common currency when teaching principles that must be easily recalled. Adding a fourth, fifth or sixth idea increases complexity and reduces retention. This is especially true in a crisis.

The best possible training will fall short if it's misunderstood or cannot be recalled in the heat of the moment.

Lock Out, Get Out, Take Out

Employees, teachers, worshippers and concertgoers all face the risk of a mass assault. Their survival depends on their training.

This means their instructions must be crystal clear, easy to remember and adaptable to their circumstances.

For this reason, we created and exclusively teach *The Three Out Response Model*: *Lock Out, Get Out, Take Out*.

The key to the *Three Out Response Model* is its adaptability. In other words, you do not first attempt to *Lock Out*, then attempt to *Get Out* and finally fight (*Take Out*). You use any and all of these tactics when necessary and in any order.

Three people may be in the same building and face the same threat. Yet each of them may need to choose a different response. One may be able to lockdown a room. Another may be able to exit into an alley. The third may have to fight for her life. Each can choose the tactic that makes the most sense in the situation.

- **Lock Out** = Keep the intruder outside the building. If he has entered, keep him out of as many rooms as possible. Locking mechanisms, such as the Barracuda[62], can make it nearly impossible for an intruder to enter a room. Don't be satisfied with a locked door alone. Create redundancy by locking, layering and reinforcing room entrances.

---

[62] The Barracuda intruder defense system is manufactured by Bilco and distributed by Strategos International. Simple locking devices fortify doors that open in or out. Learn more at www.strategosintl.com/store.

- **Get Out** = If you can get away from the threat, do so. This may mean fleeing the building or an unsafe part of it. *Get Out* also means evacuating an open area, such as a lobby, cafeteria or hallway to reach a room that can be locked or secured. In that instance, you're both getting out and locking out. Leaving the building may not always be the best option. For one, you may expose yourself to an attack getting to the exit. In addition, it's better to stay put if there's the possibility of a shooter outdoors.

- **Take Out** = If you cannot safely escape or lock out the intruder, then take him out (fight back) by any means necessary. Slam a door on his head or hands, throw a chair, stab him with scissors or hold him captive with his own weapon. Your life is on the line. You may be the only barricade standing between children, churchgoers or co-workers. Are there people in your life worth living for? If so, you owe it to them to fight. If we're going to be defeated (and let's hope and pray we won't), then let's go down fighting. Those who fight back increase their chances of living for another day. Begging and pleading with attackers only incites their twisted desire to victimize.

Lock Out, Get Out, Take Out does not prescribe an order of responses. It presents three actions that can be taken as needed and in any order. For example, if an intruder has already breached the building – or worse, your room – your only option may be to *Take Out*. If everyone can safely exit before the shooter enters, then *Get Out* would be your first option.

What if word got out that you had a chance to protect your children or employees and did nothing?

Lock Out and lockdown

There's a lockdown somewhere in the United States every week. A typical lockdown occurs when gunshots are reported near a school. Just to be safe, they batten down the hatches. We recommend this approach. Better safe than sorry.

Undoubtedly, some may object to a lockdown. Why make a fuss? What if word gets out that you had an emergency?

Conversely, what if word got out that you had a chance to protect your children or employees and did nothing?

The goal of a lockdown is to prevent an intruder from entering the building. If he gets inside, a lockdown prevents him from accessing individual rooms.

Getting your workplace into lockdown mode doesn't happen without training. Decisions that must be made ahead of time include:

- Who determines when to institute a lockdown and how it will be communicated?

- What should you do once the doors are locked?

- Who determines and announces when the lockdown is over?

In a worst-case scenario, an intruder may enter a building before a lockdown can be fully implemented. This is when *Lock Out, Get Out, Take Out* goes into action.

The Three Out Response Model
Lock Out, Get Out, Take Out

You can use any of the Three Outs at any time. There is no prescribed order. If you can safely get out, do so. If it's better to stay put, then Lock Out. If an intruder invades your room, then it's time to Take Out (fight). Do what you need to do, when you need to do it.

LOCK OUT

Lock Out means keeping the intruder outside your building. If the facility is breached, then keep the intruder out of your room. Never be satisfied with a locked door. Lock, layer, reinforce and turn off the lights.

GET OUT

If you can get away from the threat, do so. This means fleeing the building or an unsafe part of it. If you don't know where the shooter is, or if a shooter could be outside, it's better to Lock Out behind a locked, layered and reinforced door.

TAKE OUT

Take Out means fighting for your life. Attackers aren't used to being resisted, even if it's with a thrown shoe, purse or textbook. Stun them and stop them with whatever improvised weapons are at your disposal. Lives depend on it.

The Three Outs in action

Monday • 8:57 a.m.

It's not the morning supervisor Karen Welch had in mind. Still stirring the creamer into her first cup of coffee, her phone begins buzzing frantically. First it's repeated text messages. When she sets down her coffee to pick up her phone, it rings.

On the other end is Marcus from accounting. *But he's not in accounting.*

"I'm in the parking lot and Bree's husband just pulled up," he says. "You told us there's a restraining order against him and to alert everyone if he entered the property."

"Thank you. Now go ahead and drive away," responds Karen. "Get out of here."

She immediately instructs a staff member to dial 911 and then picks up the office phone to announce a lockdown.

9:00 a.m.

Jacob, Bree's husband, had made a bee-line to the front door and entered the building. It was too late to lock him outside, but there was still time to secure interior doors.

Karen picks up the company-wide phone system to announce an intruder alert and tells everyone to lock down.

9:01 a.m.
Workers flee hallways and unsecured rooms for safer spaces. They scramble to close doors, bolt locks, move furniture and switch off lights.

9:03 a.m.
Jacob is reduced to pounding on the door of the finance department where his wife works.

"Bree! Where are you? I just want to talk!"

Bree's shaken, but secure, out of the line of sight and the line of fire.

9:04 a.m.
Jacob wanders the hallways rattling door handles. Is he armed? Did he merely want to talk to his wife? Or to kill everyone?

9:05 a.m.
Frustrated, Jacob leaves the building and walks toward his car. Is he leaving? Or getting firepower from his trunk?

9:07 a.m.
Jacob drives away. But as he leaves the parking lot, his vehicle is surrounded by responding officers. As they draw their weapons, Jacob raises his hands in the air. He's arrested and removed from the scene.

How did this scenario work in terms of *Lock Out, Get Out, Take Out?*

Employees' first response was to *Lock Out*. Since Jacob didn't break into any rooms, they did not need to physically confront him (*Take Out*).

But should employees have fled the scene (*Get Out*)? Not in this scenario. Information was limited. If he were armed, Jacob may have opened fire on people as they left the building. Employees were relatively safe in their locked and barricaded rooms.

Police ultimately handled the *Take Out* part of the equation.

You could rewrite this story in many different ways and still employ *The Three Out Response Model* to deal with the threat.

If Jacob would have entered the building and attacked the receptionist, then employees would have needed to *Take Out*. While the struggle was in process, others could have left the building (*Get Out*) or secured themselves behind closed doors (*Lock Out*).

The model supplies three simple, easy-to-recall options. In a crisis, you choose the response that makes the most sense in your circumstance.

Calling 911 and cooperating with police
Although we've stated you must be prepared to do more than dial 911, calling the emergency number is critical. Call

it as soon as possible after other emergency priorities have been completed. Be ready to make your call productive.

Give the operator as much information as possible, including the location and number of shooters. If you are able, describe the attackers and their weapons. It's also helpful if you know how many employees and visitors are on site.

When officers arrive they have a unique challenge: identifying the bad guy. You can help by exhibiting calm and following police orders. Raise your hands, spread your fingers and make no sudden movements.

The first officers to arrive will not immediately treat the injured. Their mission is to stop the threat. Emergency medics will enter after police secure the area. Since the task of caring for the wounded may fall to you, we recommend getting trained in crisis casualty care. It provides personnel with the knowledge to treat wounds and save lives.

Once employees have reached a safe location, officers will keep them there until the situation is under control and all witnesses have been identified.

At Strategos, we hope you never have to use these skills in a real-life scenario. But in case you do, be ready to *Get Out, Lock Out, Take Out* and call 911.

CHAPTER 11
After the Attack

It's not over when it's over. Make sure your organization can survive a tragedy.

"Rule of survival: Pack your own parachute."
— T.L. Hakala

If – God forbid – your workplace is savaged by an active shooter, what appears like the end may only be the beginning.

Once police release all employees from the scene and the last squad car pulls away, the next chapter of the attack will begin.

"It's never really over," according to insurer McGowan Program Administrators. "The impact of an active-shooter event lingers for years. Families and co-workers struggle to heal after losing loved ones. Businesses lose revenue and consider relocating. Attorneys file lawsuits to recapture monetary losses."[63]

You need Plan B

It's impossible to predict exactly how workplace violence will impact your business. *But there will be an impact.*

---

[63] McGowan Program Administrators: "What Happens in the Aftermath of an Active Shooter Situation?" https://bit.ly/2C2oofL

"Planning is an unnatural process; it is much more fun to do something. And the nicest thing about not planning is that failure comes as a complete surprise; rather than being proceeded by a period of worry and depression."

– Sir John Harvey-Jones

You have two choices: Plan for business continuity before the event or after the event.

Which approach do you think will be more successful?

Nuts and bolts

It won't be long after the dust has settled that you must face the question, "How, when and where do we get work done?"

Although customers and constituents will certainly empathize with your plight, at some point they must pay their bills, make their purchases and ship their goods.

In the immediate aftermath of the attack, you need a plan to continue functioning while your facility is processed as a crime scene.

Depending on your type of business, that may mean employees work from home. Or it may mean temporarily renting a facility or outsourcing work.

In addition, you need a plan to address:

- How employees will get counseling and trauma care
- Replacing employees who choose not to return
- Media inquiries and crisis communications

"But will we be paid?"

After the smoke clears and emergency needs are met, employees will begin wondering if they're still going to be paid, notes the Society for Human Resource Management (SHRM). Workplaces need to be ready to address security and trauma, but also a host of post-attack operational questions.[64]

SHRM cites the example of Hartford Distributors, a Connecticut company that lost eight employees to an active shooter in 2010.[65]

The small business had limited resources, so local law enforcement asked crisis counselors and ministers to step up and support workers and their families.

Although, in this instance, community support was strong, it's better to have a plan in place beforehand.

Mental health support is critical immediately following an attack, but it cannot end there. Support must be ongoing. Consider military personnel who experience Post-Traumatic Stress Disorder (PTSD). They may battle its

---

[64] SHRM: "After an Active Shooter." https://bit.ly/2EHUbVM
[65] CNN: "Gunman 'cold as ice' before killing 8 in workplace shooting spree" https://cnn.it/2R2QECn

symptoms for a lifetime, not merely months after returning from the battlefield.

Family support

Since the workplace does not function in isolation, employers must also be ready to respond to the needs of workers' families. These can include:

- Providing information about the well-being and status of employees.

- Reunifying family members separated by the attack.

- Returning personal belongings to employees and their families.

- Holding a memorial service.

Anniversaries

One-month and annual anniversaries of the attack can trigger stress in employees, surviving family members and the community. Companies can't turn a blind eye to these dates and need to proactively anticipate the needs of employees. In addition, taking the opportunity to remember those lost or injured is the humane and right thing to do.

Workplaces also need to be ready to facilitate visits from former employees, friends and family who will benefit from the support of others.

"A business continuity planner is more powerful than all the king's horses and all the king's men, because with a plan in place we can put Humpty Dumpty back together again."
– Doug Rezner

Media and communications

Depending on the scope of the event, media interest may be global. In addition, you'll need to communicate to specific constituencies who each have different needs for information. These could include employees, customers, vendors and community leaders. All will have needs that won't be satisfied by media reports.

If your company is large enough to have a media liaison, that person needs to be thoroughly briefed on your emergency response plan. You also need a backup if your media contact is injured or unavailable. If your business has no media liaison, consider contracting for this service beforehand.

Not only do you want to keep the community informed, you want to do it in a way that avoids legal liabilities. For example, you are limited in what you can say about individual employees' actions and medical status. You must avoid statements that could impede a law enforcement investigation. And, if your company is publicly held, you certainly don't want to destroy its stock price with careless words.

Crisis response media relations is not the place for a PR newcomer to experience baptism by fire. Leave it to the pros so you can focus on recovery.

Is it worth it all?
If all of this seems daunting, it is. But is there any other choice? As we've stated earlier, we take the threat of hurricanes, tornados and fires seriously. The risk of an attack is equally real. All crisis events require a recovery plan, whether the turmoil begins with a lightning bolt or a gun.

If you have a business, school or church worth running, then you have one worth saving and recovering.

CHAPTER 12

It's Your Turn: Seize the Day

What you do next could be the most important decision you ever make.

"Expect the best, plan for the worst and prepare to be surprised." – Denis Waitley

If you've made it this far in this book, you're serious about crisis response and recovery. You're one of a rare breed and we commend you.

We want to caution you to avoid two extremes. The first is to toss this book on the shelf as a good idea for a rainy day. The second is to run yourself into the ground trying to implement all of it in one month's time.

How, then, should you proceed?

Start at the top

If you're the owner or CEO, you don't need approval. You can begin. However, if you must persuade the owner or a board, you'll need to proceed carefully.

Assess where key stakeholders stand on the issue of crisis response and recovery. Has someone tried to create a plan before? If so, what happened? There is no need to run into the same wall a previous proposal hit. Instead, take a different approach.

If you're not sure where leadership stands, begin by asking questions. What are their real concerns? Are they financial? Do they have bad information? Is there a key relational conflict that might prevent progress?

Although you don't want to waste time, consider your work to be a process, not a quick fix.

"Emergency preparedness is a team sport."
– Eric Whitaker

Get a team
Once you have approval for some or all of a plan, you'll need to gather a team around you.

There is simply too much work for one person to handle. In addition, disciplines ranging from manufacturing to human resources to insurance and security are all involved. You don't know enough to succeed on your own.

Your plan will be more complete and your organization will be better prepared with a team.

Don't give up
Even with the most supportive leadership and an enthusiastic team, your journey will be a long-distance run and not a sprint. Set short-term, intermediate and long-term goals. Then check them off and celebrate victories along the way.

How we can help

Strategos International exists to help organizations counter and prevail over workplace threats. We've trained more than 150,000 personnel in 15 countries since 2002.

We evaluate facilities and security plans, train employees and provide on-site protection for high-risk terminations and other volatile workplace issues.

You've got a job to do, whether it's processing grain, educating the next generation or teaching spiritual values. Let us focus on security so you can keep your focus where it belongs.

Thank you for reading and for your commitment to a safe workplace.

Sincerely,
Vaughn Baker, president: vaughn@strategosintol.com

Mark Warren, executive vice president: mark@strategosintl.com

More ways to reach us

- www.strategosintl.com
- www.facebook.com/Team.Strategos
- twitter.com/teamstrategos

Additional Resources: *PREVAIL!*™

PREVAIL!™ is a unique active-shooter training experience that moves instruction out of the realm of the abstract and into the reality of the personal.

Sollah Interactive commissioned professional actors, renovated an empty office building and sought the expert counsel of Strategos' President Vaughn Baker. The result is something that redefines the concept of a training video. In this gripping drama, real people face threats of life and death in the 9-to-5 grind of their workplace. Some rise to the occasion. Others don't.

Many active-shooter trainings are centered around complex sets of principles that lack relevance to reality. *PREVAIL!*™ is built around *The Three Out Response Model* developed by Strategos International.

The curriculum is called *PREVAIL!*™ because merely surviving is defensive and can lead to a victim's mindset. PREVAILING! is about taking action.

PREVAIL!™ was designed for clarity and simplicity. Organizations can use 1-, 2- and 3-hour training options. Instruction begins with the dramatic video, then shifts to training, discussion and opportunities for application in the workplace. Additional material is also available for managers to help inform and prepare their teams to discuss crisis planning.

Pricing is flexible and is based on the number of participants and the delivery model.

In addition to the video training, Strategos offers a live, on-site *PREVAIL!*™ Two-Day Champions Experience and advanced training and consulting.

Please contact us to discuss the program that is right for you.

Learn more at www.strategosintl.com/prevail

Words of praise for *PREVAIL!*™

"*PREVAIL!*™, created by Strategos International and Sollah Interactive, has been well received throughout our organization. Employee feedback indicates the video accurately portrays the reality of a critical event, from the serious tone to the detailed subject matter. The production quality is excellent, which helps to engage and educate the viewer. Employees also appreciate the tip cards, indicating this will improve retention. Strategos and Sollah provide extraordinary service and products, working with us diligently to ensure our organization and employees receive top-notch training."

Daniel Baird, Security Coordinator, INTRUST Bank N.A.

13072390R00071

Made in the USA
Middletown, DE
23 November 2018